# 숨은 꽃

# The hidden flower

# 1

## 정송전 한영시집

Korean-English Poems Collection of Jeong Song Jeon

을지출판공사

## ■ 자서自序

삶의 다양한 모습과 고단한 숨결이 시의 눈을 틔우고 오만 가지 허드레 잡념까지도 내게로 와서 시가 되었을 때, 그것은 돌올한 내 시의 성취라면 성취라고 감히 자부한다.

나는 내 시집 〈내 이렇게 살다가〉의 자서에 다음과 같이 적은 적이 있다.

'나의 여정은 분명 저녁나절쯤이지만 나의 시는 아직 새벽이다. 그래서 하염없이 회안에 젖는다.'

내 삶이 어느 날 느닷없이 내가 아닌 것처럼 비춰지기도 했으며 삶의 질곡이 부질없이 그리움으로 다가오기도 했음을 고백한다. 그러나 그럴 때마다 내 삶의 심지를 곧추세우는 의연한 '여유' 가 나를 건져 내기도 했다. 이것이 내 시의 이력이자 본령이라는 것을 나는 잊지 않는다.

끝으로, 이 영문시집 펴내는데 있어 아내(신미자)와 아들(정주헌) 노고가 컸음을 밝혀 둔다.

2022. 5. 10

지은이 정송전

## ▪ The Preface of the Poet

When the various aspects and the weary breath of life put forth a bud of poetry and even tens of thousands of miscellaneous trivia thoughts come to me and become poetry, if I can call it, I dare to say that's the accomplishment of my outstanding poetry.

I once wrote the following in my essay for my collection of poems, 〈Living like this〉.

'My journey is certainly about the evening, but my poem is still dawn. So, I get soaked in endless remorse.'

I confess that one day my life suddenly felt like it wasn't me, and that life's ordeal came to me in vain longing. But every time that happened, the resolute 'Composure' that made my life upright, saved me. I do not forget that this is the history and the original characteristic of my poetry.

To conclude, I would like to acknowledge the efforts of my wife (Mija Shin) and son (Jooheon Jeong) in writing this English poem collection.

2022. 5. 10

Author Jeong Song jeon

## 차례



### 제 1 부 헤아릴 수 없는 삶의 진실
### Part 1 The Immeasurable Truth of Life

## 제2부 꽃으로 피어나는 사랑과 이별
## Part 2 Love and Farewell Blooming Flowers

차례

## 제3부 그리움 되작거리는 고향 찬가
## Part 3 The Haunting Hymns of My Hometown

## 제 4 부 따뜻한 중심에 이르는 길

## Part 4 The Road to the Warm Center

# 제 1 부 Part 1

# 헤아릴 수 없는 삶의 진실

# The Immeasurable Truth of Life

겨울나무는
제 촉수를
가슴 안으로 뻗는다

푸르기만 한 하늘
그 아래서.
-「겨울나무 · 1」 중에서

A winter tree
Stretches its tentacles
Into the chest.

A sky with the only blue
Beneath it.
- The part of「A winter tree · 1」

# 갈 등

친정에 간 아내에게도
밤은 이내
연민의 이슬을 내린다.

마당 가득 채색된 달무리가
회한의 그늘로 파고들 때면
깨물어 둔 사과빛 심장 속으로
어물어물 깃드는 그대 숨소리.

# Struggle

Even my wife who went to her parents' home
The night soon
Sheds dewdrops of compassion.

Fully in the yard, when the colored halo,
Penetrates in the shade of remorse
Into the apple-colored heart of bitten,
Sloppily your breathing is covered.

# 삶

성애처럼 입김에도 흩어지는 것.

풋과일 속 색소로 숨어 있는 것.

손바닥에 파닥이는 꽃잎 같은 것.

# Life

Scattered in breathing like a frost.

Hid as colorings inside a green fruit.

Petaled as a fluttering in the palm.

# 나 홀로

꽃도 없고 바람도 없이
시공을 떠돌며
애련의 눈망울로 익혀야 할
그 무엇이 없다 할지언정
조금도 이상할 것이 없다.

너의 고통을 내 안에
촘촘히 심어 놓고
혼자서 벽지를 발랐다
가랑잎에 막힌 수채구를 뚫고
쓰레기로 밤을 태웠다.

푸른 들녘 한가운데
달빛이 쏟아져도
그리움 지우며
빨래판에 손을 문질러도
방황의 끝은 알 수 없었다.

# Alone

Without flowers and winds
Wandering through time and space
What I need to learn with a plaintive glance,
Even there is no such like thing,
Nothing to be weird.

Your pain is inside the mine
I planted it densely,
Pasted the wallpaper by myself,
Drilled the drain blocked by fallen leaves,
Burned the night with trash.

In the middle of a blue field
Even the moonlight pours
I was erasing longings,
Even rubbing hands on the washing board
I couldn't tell about the end of the wandering.

자유도 니글거리고
갈등마저 심심하다보니
밤이 대낮으로 물구나무 서 있었다
그 무엇이 파문을 일으키며
홀로 지내는 세상을 뒤척이는가.

Because freedom was greasy
Conflict was tedious
The night was standing on its hands like in the daytime
What is causing the stir and
Tossing and turning the world of living alone?

# 가족 나들이

우리 가족의 나들이었다
겨울을 이겨낸 나목들처럼
움틀 게 있어서 신났다.

뽐낼 것도 없는
갯벌에 싸인 대부도로
우리 가족은 나들이었다.

출렁이는 바다를 나눠 가지며
우리 가족은
자유가 고여 있는
낡은 관사 마당에
나들이를 심었다.

나는 그 그림자 속에
오늘을 환하게 덧칠해야 한다.

# A family outing

It was my family outing
Like bare trees that have survived the winter,
I was excited to have something sprouts.

With nothing to boast one,
Covered with tideland, to Daebu Island
My family was an outing.

We shared the floating sea
My family,
There was stagnant freedom,
In the old yard of the official residence
We planted our outing.

Inside its shadow
I must paint today brightly.

# 내 이렇게 살다가

이미 죽어서 내다버린 이름 모를 분재 하나 주워다가
빈 화분에 심어 놓고
뿌리 내리고 잎이 나기를 바라면서
제법 떨림 같은 사랑을 퍼부었다.

포근한 햇살 가까이
줄기를 가만히 만져보니 화끈거리는 것 같다
마디 켜켜이 보조개 그늘 속에
세포들이 땀을 흘리며 헉헉대는 것 같다
그래, 분명히 속살을 여미는구나 싶은데
얼마나 사무치며 꿈꾸어 온 것일까.

내 영혼은 두 개로 늘어났다
참으로 신기한 나의 향수이다
죽었다가 다시 살아나고
꽃피워 하늘에 도래질 할 때면
얼마나 자비롭고 창창한 차림이냐.

# I would live like this

I picked up an unknown bonsai that was already dead, thrown,
Planted it in an empty pot,
Hoped it would take root and sprout,
Poured out my loves like almost trembling.

Closely at warm sunshine
Carefully touching its stem makes me glow
In the shadow of dimples between layered joints,
Cells might make the sound of a tough breath
Right, seems like opening its bare skin definitely
How long have you been dreaming of it desperately?

My soul has grown into two
It's my nostalgia like mysteries
Died and survived again,
Bloomed and shaking its head toward the sky
How generous and promising appearance!

내 이렇게 살다가
혈육처럼 상봉하리
초록빛 매무새로 들녘에 서서
잊고 지낸 사람의 가슴을 열어보리.

I would live like this,
Meet it as a family with blood,
Standing on the field with a greenish dress look,
Will open its breast of a forgotten one.

# 겨울나무 · 1

가지마다 내밀한 꿈을
저장하는 동안

매운 바람
눈보라

겨울나무는
제 촉수를
가슴 안으로 뻗는다.

푸르기만 한 하늘
그 아래서.

# A winter tree · 1

Inner secret dreams in each branch
While storing them

A fierce wind
A blizzard

A winter tree
Stretches its tentacles
Into the chest.

A sky with the only blue
Beneath it.

# 어느 별리

비 오는 간이역에서
듣는 기적은
한 마리 새.

차창에 노을을 뭉개 놓은 이는
누구일까.

바람 속으로 어리는
후조候鳥의 꿈.

# A certain separation

At the rainy simple station
A miracle to hear
A bird.

The one who crushes the sunset on the car window
Who would it be?

Dimly visible through the wind,
Dream of a migratory bird.

# 연가

푸르디푸른
떨림이었다.

멈칫 멈칫대는
망설임이었다.

넘치고 넘치는 갈구여.

# A love song

Bluest blue
It was a flutter.

Hesitantly hesitate
It was hesitancy.

Abundantly overflowing, an ardent wish, it is.

# 바람은

바람은 살아서 어둠일 수도 있고
이슬로 매달린 번뇌이기도 하다.

풍상을 휘젓고 산다는 것이
나를 조금씩 지워가고 있음일까.

물 위에
바람이 맨발로 서 있다.

살아 있는 모든 형상들은
몇 마디 말만 남겨 놓고
바람 속으로 사라져간다.

참 이상한 일이지
예사롭게 눈에 비취는 것마다
그대로 바람과 비유된다.

이제는 모진 말, 눈빛을
마음에 새기지 않도록 한다.

# The wind is

The wind could be living darkness
Also dewy hanging agony.

Living life with disturbing hardships is
Erasing myself gradually, maybe.

On the water
The wind is standing barefoot.

All living shapes are
Left with few words,
Faded through the wind.

What a strange thing!
Everything which reflects ordinary in my eyes,
Is likened to the wind as it is.

Now with sharp words, looks,
Never would be kept in mind.

# 나의 섬

끝내 일어서지 못하는 섬
섬은 마냥 어지럼을 달랜다.

아무 데고
언제이고
여긴 기다림이 없다.

오직 바람에 날리는 구름
파도에 씻기는 그리움이
가까이서 휘날리는 손길이다.

나의 섬은
끝날 이후에도 그대로
혼자서 출렁이기만 하겠지.

# My island

An island that eventually fails to stand,
Forever soothes own dizziness.

Anywhere
Whenever
Here never exist waiting.

Flying clouds by winds only
Washing longings by waves are,
Flapping close touches of hands.

My island will just
Splashing alone
After the end day.

# 호숫가

바람이 별들을 털어 내니
호수에 별들이 가득하다.

하늘 속에 숨어 있는
간절함을 어찌하랴.

누구에게나 따로
남길 것은 남겨 두자.

모든 걸 털어놓고
빈 손으로 가게 하고
돌아오길 기원해 본다.

## Lakeside

When the wind sweeps off stars
The lake is full of stars.

The desperate hope that is hidden in the sky,
How could handle it?

To everyone
Let's leave something to be left.

Let everything empty and
Let them go empty-handed
I wish they would come back.

# 가을 길

파란 하늘에도
길이 있다.

몽롱한 기억으로
내달리는 소리를 듣는다.

한여름 무지개 아래서
꽃을 가꾸던 집중이 뒤돌아뵌다.

달과 별의 마당에
시련이랄까, 염원을 걸어 놓고

가을 길은
혼자서 자기를 버티고 서서
하늘을 닦는다.

# The autumn road

Even in the blue sky
There' s a road.

In a dreamy memory
Hears a running sound.

Under the midsummer rainbow
The focused mind of caring flowers is seen from behind.

In the yard of the moon and stars,
Hangs an ordeal or wishes and

The autumn road
Stands and sustains itself,
Wipes the sky.

# 봄을 향하여

성급함이야
목련을 당해낼 수 있을까
잎을 떨구면서
벌써 봄눈을 내밀어
겨울 나더니

햇빛이 바람결에
시린 그대로
하얀 시포屍布자락
하늘로 돌돌 말아 올리다가
머금은 미소 그냥 고와서
달빛에 비추어
밤을 지새면

화들짝 꽃잎 펼치려
밤잠 설치는 그대.

# Toward spring

Regarding hastiness
Nothing could cope with the magnolia
With dropping its leaves
Already hands out a sprout of spring then,
Spending the winter

In the sunshine beside winds
Cold as it is
With a white winding-sheet,
Rolling up into the sky
Just feeling the pretty smile it has,
Reflecting it in the moonlight,
Staying up all night

For spreading its petals out,
Unable to sleep well, it's you.

# 거울 속

거울 속에서
한 사내가 걸어 나온다.

어디로 가야만
아껴 간직해 온 한마디 말을
나부낄 수 있을까.

밤의 장막을 움켜쥐고
소리결은 그림으로 자리잡는다.

골짜기 깊은 곳에는
꽃대에 아득한 불빛이 서려 있겠지.

오랜 거울 안에
번지는 노을 너머론
무슨 바람이 휘날리고 있을까.

새 한 마리 날개깃 소리
어둠 속으로 비껴간다.

# In the mirror

In the mirror
A man walks out.

Where should I go
To say away
A word I've cherished?

Crabbing the night's curtain,
The layer of sound is settled as a picture.

Deep in the valley
There must be a dim light on the flower stalk.

In the old mirror
Beyond the spreading sunset
What kind of wind is fluttering?

The flying sound of a bird's wing,
It slips into the dark.

# 메아리

오죽하면
내가 시를 쓰겠나.

목화처럼 하얗게
파도로 넘실대다가
어찌하여
미망迷妄의 꽃을 심겠나.

인생 절단날 것만 같아서
지난 것 듬뿍 머금어

구름 햇살에 녹아
수평선 너머 화들짝 핀
꽃밭을 찾아와
이 숭얼스런 꿈을 뒤집어 보겠나.

# An echo

How desperately do I,
Become to write a poem?

As white as a cotton plant
I was surging as the waves,
How do I,
Become to plant an elusive flower?

Feel like that my life was about to be cut,
Wearing with plenty of past things and

Melted by the sunshine of clouds
Flowered wildly over the horizon
Come to find a flower field,
Become to turn this noisy dream upside down.

# 제 2 부 Part 2

# 꽃으로 피어나는 사랑과 이별

# Love and Farewell Blooming Flowers

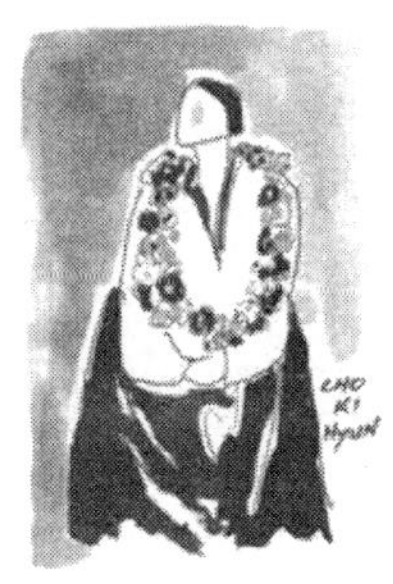


하늘이 바다에 내려와
밤새도록 달빛에 젖다가
파도로 부서지는가.
낯선 대면이라
안개 너울 수줍음 가린 채
꼼짝 않고 서 있다.
-「독도」 중에서

The sky is descending to the ocean,
Soaked all night by the moonlight
Is it crashed into the waves?

As a strange encounter
Hiding the shyness of waving fog,
It stands motionlessly.
- The part of「Dokdo」

# 꽃

달이 지고
별이 삭은
그늘 속에
다시 별자리를 닦는다.

그대 속살에
스민 온갖 색소色素.

어느 날 가까이
새벽을 오려내면서

거기 서 있는 그대로
신부新婦가 되는
그대.

# A flower

The moon is set
The star is rotten
In the shade,
I wipe the star sign again.

Into your bare skin
All kinds of colorings permeate.

One day closely,
Cutting out the dawn

Just like you're standing there
To become a bride,
You.

# 숨은 꽃

어수선한 날 비를 맞으며
가을 아침을 나온다.

잠시 눈을 감고
코스모스의 내밀한 부름을 듣는다
그에겐 비밀이 없으랴.

꽃이 아닌 내가
시작과 끝이 없는 미망의 길목에
나를 풀어 놓는다.

이슬 머금은 지평에서
이대로 외면해야겠다.

그 단발머리의 물새는
오늘 혼자
꽃의 모양을 헤집어 놓고
부질없는 비밀을 캐고 있겠지.

# The hidden flower

In the rain on an unstable day
I come out in the autumn morning.

Shortly close eyes,
I hear the inner call from a cosmos
Probably it has no secrets.

Though I'm not a flower,
On the street corner of delusion with no beginning and no end
I am releasing myself.

On the dewy horizon
I will turn my face away as this state.

That waterfowl with short hair
Alone today,
Will disturb the shape of a flower,
Be digging up useless secrets.

# 어떤 꽃

그리운 때에 뉘우침이
요동을 치며
가슴 속으로 힘겹다.

마주한 나의 얼굴빛은 가면 속에서
부끄럽고 무안했고
빛이란 빛은 모두
나를 허뜨려 분산시킨다.

서로를 가늠한 흔적 남기고
여백을 남긴 채
스러져가는 형상이다.

이제는 어떠한 아픔도 잊고
태양을 바래 손길 펼친다.

# A certain flower

On a longing day, remorse is
Shaking and
A burden to my mind.

The complexion I face is inside the mask,
Ashamed and embarrassed
Every single light,
Breaks down and scatters me.

Leaving the trace of each other's guessing
Leaving blanks,
It's a vanishing form.

Now I forget any pain,
Spread out my hands toward the sun.

# 풀 꽃

하필이면
시멘트 틈새에 끼어 피었나.

제 그림자만큼 비켜나면
꽃밭에 꽃이 되련마는

별나게 살아도
결국, 한 세상일진대

고개 돌려 외면한 채
별빛에 젖은 그 눈망울

너는 다만
풀꽃으로 피었구나.

# A wildflower

Of all things, you're
Flowered in a crevice of cement.

If you move as far away as your shadow,
Could be a flower in a garden

Even if you live unusually
In the end, you live only once

Turning your face away,
Those eyes wet with starlight

You just,
Bloomed in a field.

# 찔레꽃

달빛이 나뭇가지로 찔레넝쿨을 후려쳐
밤새
무논에 찔레 꽃잎이 하얗게 널렸다.

둑 가에 하얀 뿌리로 매달려
장마사태에 겁먹은 찔레

집에 오는 길에
한 뿌리 뽑아들고 와
함께 살게 되었다.

시작과 끝을
한 울타리 안에서 지내는 오늘

내 마음의 강바닥에
찔레꽃은 하염없이 지고지고
하루가 저무는 황혼녘은
붉기만 하다.

# A multiflora rose

The moonlight flipped the vines with branches of multiflora
All night long
The multiflora petals were strewn white on the rice field.

Hanging with white roots on the bankside
Scared of the rainy season, a multiflora rose

On my way home
Pulled up one root and hold,
Become to live together.

From beginning to end
Being in the same fence today

On the riverbed of my heart
It falls and falls endlessly,
In the twilight of the day
It's nothing but rosy red.

# 바람을 머금은 꽃

달도 별도 호수 속으로 잠긴다.
오늘밤 나도
바람을 머금은 꽃이 된다.

이제 돌아갈 수 없는 뒷자리를 바라보면
꽃은 바람의 모습으로 서 있다.

멀고 가까운 하늘 아래
꽃 아닌 게 어디 있겠는가.

저만치 함께 서 있는 나무끼리
어깨를 짚어 어루만지며
한마디 말은 끝내
못하고 마나 보다.

# A windy flower

The moon and stars sink into the lake
Tonight, I also
Become a flower with the wind.

Now looking at the behind place which never can go back
The flower stands in the form of wind.

Under the sky far and near
Where is something that is not a flower?

A distant, trees are standing together
Touching each one's shoulder
A word in the end,
Never might be said.

# 동백꽃

출렁이는 뱃고동소리에
부두는 앓았다.

그대 하늘이
해조음을 가득 담아
부두를 떠났다.

푸념을 묻어 둔 채
바위 틈새로 의지하여 온
모진 근성이여.

거만한 몸짓도 아닌
검버섯 핀 몸짓으로
갯바람에 삭혀 온 그리움이여.

그대 발등에 물거품으로 고여
가슴 속 깊이 입술을 대고
물새들의 시샘을 듣는다.

허기진 파도는
자락지어 퍼지고
뱃머리엔 동백꽃이 화안했다.

## Camellia flowers

From the surging sound of a foghorn
The dock suffers.

Your sky with
Holding fully the sound of the sea,
Has left the dock.

Buried a complaint
Relied on a rock crevice,
Tough patience, it is.

Not an arrogant gesture
But a gesture with age spots,
Rotten by sea breezes, it's longing.

Reserved as a bubble on your top of the foot
Touched on lips deep in the heart,
Listening to the water birds' jealousy.

Hungry waves
Spread out with a melody
Camellia flowers brightly bloomed on the bow.

# 박 꽃

매품 팔고
돌아온 밤에
달빛은
앙가슴 속 같았던 박꽃이었대.

[흥부 아내 하는 말이
형제간이라 잊었소,
엄동설한 추운 날에
곽 속에 들어도 못 잊겠소.]

눈물 그렁그렁
먼 산이 다가와
젖은 바가지에 담긴
그림자.

어매 서방님
어찌 이 모진 찰랑 세월
잊고 살잔 말이어요.

# A gourd flower

Selling of being beaten then,
On his return night
The moonlight
Was like a gourd flower in the middle of the chest.

[Heungbu's wife said,
Did you forget about it because he's your brother?
In this severe winter
I won't forget it even when I will be in a coffin.]

With tears in its eyes
A distant mountain approaches
A wet bowl has
The shadow.

Oh, my husband
How could we forget,
This whipping tough time?

* Translator Comment: This episode of the poem came from Heungbujeon, one of the traditional Korean stories. Heungbu, who was driven out of the house by his bad elder brother Nolbu, was poor enough to be beaten on behalf of others and feed his family in return.

# 목 련

솜털 망울로
겨울 나더니
거친 숨결로
벙으러진 앙가슴.

하늘로 치올려
돌돌 휘감긴 치마폭에
어룽지는 수액.

바람이 다가와
하얀 촉감을 씻는다
햇빛 속으로 가득
그리움이 벙글어
그리움이 벙글어.

# A cotton flower

With a fluffy bud
After the winter
With a tough breath,
Opened the middle of the chest.

Soaring skyward
With a skirt wrapped around,
Mottled by wood sap.

The winds approach and
Wash the white touch's feeling
Full of sunlight
The longings are in bud
The longings are in bud.

# 겨울 개나리

비워있는 것이
채워진 것 같은 느낌이다.

완행열차 손님으로 기다리다
세상 일 모두 털어 봄을 샀다.

아득한 이별 어디쯤
그 속삭임의 표정이다.

비늘눈으로 하늬바람 앞에서 숨죽이더니
언뜻 자줏빛
언뜻 푸른빛
언뜻 노란빛.

너도 세상을 감상하는지.

# A winter forsythia

The empty things
Have a feeling like to be filled.

Waited as a customer of a slow train,
Bought spring by spending all the worldly things.

Somewhere of a far farewell
That's the expression of the whisper.

Holding its breath as a bulbil in the west wind,
Swiftly purplish
Swiftly bluish
Swiftly yellowish.

Wondering if you also appreciate the world.

# 사랑과 진실

토라져 있노라면
먼저 말 걸어오는 관심
한 마디 농담에도 생기가 넘치는 미소
챙겨주기 바라는 순진한 눈빛
받기를 먼저 바라는 욕심이

만에 하나라도 세월이 좋아지면
설마 그런 날이 있겠느냐마는
손목을 잡고 떠날 줄 모르던
산안개가 지워버린 바람

이제 다시 너에게로 갈 때
이렇게 머뭇거리지 않았으면 좋으련만
흔들리는 나뭇가지에도
자기 생각은 따로 있겠지.

# Love and truth

When I am sulking,
Your interest to start talking first
Plenty of lively smiles at every joke
Innocent eyes that want to be looked after
The desire of receiving first

If the years are favorable at least cases,
That kind of day wouldn't come
The erased wind by mountain fog,
Which didn't know to leave with grabbing the wrist

Now I go back to you
I wish I don't hesitate like this
Even on a trembling twig
There's own thought separately.

# 갈대와 나비와

갈대밭을 배경하고
황혼녘에 한 마리 나비가 앉아 있다.

다가와 어둠으로 질척일 순간에
무슨 소중한 예감이었을까.

처음부터 갈대가 아니었으면서도
오늘 새삼스럽게도
갈대이고 싶다.

가슴으로 새긴 것들
최후로 차려놓고
나는 처음부터 바람과 더불었나 보다.

오목 렌즈로 햇빛을 모아쥐던 시절
실없는 눈으로 추억을 응시한다.

나비 한 마리
어디론지 바람에 날려갔다.

## The reeds and a butterfly and

In the background of the reeds
A butterfly is sitting at dusk.

At the moment when it comes near the muddy dark
What is the precious premonition?

Even though it wasn't a reed from the beginning
Anew today
A reed, I want to be.

What I carved by my heart,
Prepared it for the last moment
I might have come along with the winds.

The days when I collected sunshine by a concave lens,
I stare at memories with silly eyes.

A butterfly
Somewhere was blown away by the wind.

# 기다림과 그림자

기다림은
하루가 기울 때
땅거미가 내리는 것을 안타까워했다.

지치지 않고
신나게 내달리는 시간

잠을 자다가도
몇 번이고 눈을 떠보면
모두가 저대로들 바쁘게 지나가고
나는 그 자리 그대로였다.

내가 가꾸던 꽃은
어떤 기다림으로 피어날까.

발길을 돌려
어디론가 떠나가고 싶을 때
흔들리는 나뭇가지만 바라본다.

# The waiting and a shadow

The waiting does
When the day is tilted
Felt pity for the dusk.

Tirelessly
A rush of time with a joy

Even when I was sleeping,
When I opened my eyes again and again
Everybody was busy and passing respectively
I stayed where I was.

The flowers I was looking for
What kind of waiting will it blossom into?

Turning around my footsteps
When I want to go somewhere,
I look at just the swinging branches.

# 뒤돌아 보면

헛눈 파는 창에
박제 되어 어른대는 형상은

호박 넝쿨로 포박된
바람으로
발을 멈춘다.

꽃 대궁들이
고단한 언어로
저희끼리 귓속을 후빈다.

서풋 맺힌 이슬로
하늘이 뭉그댄다
하루가 싱겁다.

거울에 마음을 포개놓고
고단한 내 숨소리가
갇히고 만다.

# In retrospect

On the window, I am looking at distractedly
The shimmering image with a stuffed one is

Tied up with pumpkin vines
By wind,
It stopped its foot.

The great palaces of flowers are
Picking their ears between themselves
In exhausting language.

Because of dew being formed lightly
The sky is lingering
The day is insipid.

My mind is folded in the mirror
My tired breath is
Trapped there, eventually.

# 독 도

사방은 수평선
시린 바람 돌돌 말아
한 점 혈육으로 도사린 바위.

자유를 외면하고
머슴 사는 것같이 살면서도
지평을 향한 그리움은 사무치고

하늘이 바다에 내려와
밤새도록 달빛에 젖다가
파도로 부서지는가.

낯선 대면이라
안개 너울 수줍음 가린 채
끔짝 않고 서 있다.

가까이 다가가
눈물만은 애써 감춘
너처럼 나도
한 점 혈육인 섬,
섬.

# Dokdo

All sides with the horizon
After rolling chilly winds
As its flesh and blood, the rocks lurk.

Neglecting freedom,
Lived the life of a servant,
Longed for severely toward the horizon of land

The sky is descending to the ocean,
Soaked all night by the moonlight
Is it crashed into the waves?

As a strange encounter
Hiding the shyness of waving fog,
It stands motionlessly.

Get closer
Tried to hide tears
Like you, I am also
A flesh and blood,
An island.

## 제3부 Part 3

# 그리움 되작거리는 고향 찬가

# The Haunting Hymns of My Hometown

이웃들은 다 떠나고 없어도
저 혼자 색깔을 간직하고

말없이 늘
그 자리에 있다.

고향의 얼굴이다.
- 「빈 집에서」 중에서

Even all the neighbors are gone
Keeps its colors alone.

Speechlessly all the time,
Being in that place.

It's the face of my hometown.
- The Part of 「In the empty house」

# 고향 하늘

피어오른 아지랑이
현기증을 잊고 살았다.

언제나 그리움은
스러질 줄 몰랐다.

이슬 내린 풀잎 하나에도
숨소리 들릴라.

# The sky of my hometown

A rising haze
Has lived with forgetting its dizziness.

Always longings
Were never going to fall.

Even a dewy grass leaf
Afraid to hear breathing.

# 뒷모습

비 오는 거리에서
어느 말씀을 더듬어
머리말에 놓았다.

말씀대로 허황히 거리로 나와
뒤돌아 서서 바라보면
나는 항시 무너지는 그대로의 나일 뿐.

앞두고 온 하늘에서보다
무료함과 궁금함 속에서
자기를 찾는 것이 더 값질 것이다.

환경이 다르면 적응하는 법이다.
애써 변화가 없다면 무슨 의미가 있겠느냐.

뒷모습은
자기 모습으로 가는 것이다.

# The appearance from behind

On a rainy street
Remembered vaguely some word
I put it on the side of my head.

Forlornly coming out into the street as that word
Looking at it after turning around
I am always the one who collapses.

Than in the sky that I've left previously,
More in tediousness and curiosity
Finding myself there will be more valuable.

Different circumstances lead to adaptation
What does it mean if there's no change?

The appearance from behind
It's the thing which goes to own shape.

# 어느 기다림

치장했을 꽃망울도
포근한 살결 감촉도
그을린 한 조각
신음.

발돋움도
어떤 꽃의 몸짓도 아닌
끝내 알 수 없는
허공.

그래, 서성거리는 눈빛만
나로선 어차피 석상의 숨결이었다.

나의 갇힌 시간만
들꽃으로 피어 하늘거렸다.

# A certain wait

A flower bud with decoration and
The warm feeling of skin
Are the tanned pieces of
Moaning.

Not a footstep
Not any floral gesture
Not knowing in the end,
But an empty space.

Right, only a prowling look
For me, it was the breath of a stone statue anyway.

My only trapped time
Is fluttering as the blooming of wildflower.

# 저물녘에

가을의 빈 들녘에 허수아비로 서서

햇살을 골라 줍다가

호젓한 풍경이 하나둘 사라지면

저물녘 산이 손짓을 한다.

# At dusk

Standing as a scarecrow in an empty field in autumn

Picking out the chosen sunshine

If the lonely landscape disappears gradually

The mountain at dusk makes a gesture.

# 빈집에서

비록 잡초일지라도
꽃필 때를 안다.

이웃들은 다 떠나고 없어도
저 혼자 색깔을 간직하고

말없이 늘
그 자리에 있다.

고향의 얼굴이다.

# In the empty house

Even it's a nameless grass
Knows when to bloom.

Even all the neighbors are gone
Keeps its colors alone and

Speechlessly all the time,
Being in that place.

It's the face of my hometown.

# 그림자

이별이란 게
어쩌면 거품같은 거.

사랑의 그늘에 앉아
하늘을 꽃잎처럼 펼쳐도
삶의 공간은 가려지지 않는 거.

유년으로 멈춰 있는
독백의 주름치마
외출에서 돌아와 방문을 열면
인식의 꽃이 쏟아지고

그래도
이별이란 건
시선이 지워지지 않는
그림자 같은 거.

## A shadow

The farewell is
Maybe bubblelike.

Sitting in the shadow of love
Even though spread out the sky like petals
It is unable to cover the space of life.

Being a standstill in childhood
It's a wrinkled skirt of monologue
When coming back from the outside, and open the door,
The flowers of perception pour out and

Even so
The farewell is
With an indelible look
Like a shadowy something.

# 저녁 노을

저녁 노을 가운데
허수아비 그림자가 기다랗다.

한 줄기 그늘로 남아
여윈 얼굴.

먼 날을 두고
바람으로 미소짓는다.

보이지 않는 것은 모두가
잊지 않도록 이름지어진
사랑의 비유다.

# The glow of the sky at sundown

In the middle of sundown
The scarecrow has a long shadow.

Remained as a beam of shadow,
A thin face.

For a far day,
Smiles with the hope.

Every invisible thing is
Named not to be forgotten,
It's a metaphor of love.

# 향 수

차창으로 본
텃밭에 봄동이 파랗다
옷자락으로 풋내음을 일렁인다

멀고 머언 나의 방황이다

# Nostalgia

Seen through a car window
Cabbage sprouts of spring in the garden are blue
The fresh smell is agitated by the edge of clothes

Far and far, it's my wandering

# 그림자 하나 · 1

풀꽃이 벙그러진 건널목에서
나는 신호를 기다린다
눈을 감고도 가려낼 수 있는 밤
낮
이들은 자만하고 부활한다.

오늘따라 더 처절하게 엿보이는 무게
묵혀버린 꿈의 날개로부터
한겹 껍질을 벗기면
저렇듯 빛나게 고여 있는 물거품.

가득한 소음을 덮으며
마냥 고통이어야 한다.

# One shadow · 1

On the crossroad where wildflowers flourish
I am waiting for the signal
The night that can be chosen with closing eyes
Daytime
They are arrogant and resurrected.

The burden desperately reveals today
From the wings of an unused dream
Once it's peeled off the skin,
How sparkling water foams like that!

Covering the full of noise
It has to be just a pain.

# 여름밤 풍경화

산 그림자 내리면
시골 마당 모깃불을 태운다.

수숫대 밭 너머로
채색된 연기가 피어오른다.

바람 한 점 없이 심심한 나날
푸른 여름밤의 공간에 나앉았다.

저마다 비슷한 거리에서
어디로 몰려가는지
나는 항상 낯설기만 하다.

텅 빈 하늘에
하나 둘 팔매질만 해댔다.

# A landscape painting on a summer night

When the mountain shadow falls,
I kindle a fire for driving mosquitoes out in the country yard.

Over the millet field
The colored smoke is rising.

In the windless, boring day
Seating outside the blue summer night.

At a similar distance of their own
Where they're going
I am always unfamiliar with it.

In the hollow of the sky
I threw one or two stones.

# 별의 독백

빛의 속도로 천년을 가도
밤하늘의 별은 총총하다는데
저 별이 나에게 천년을 달려왔는가
내가 전생부터 천년을 다가왔는가.

하마
내세에까지 한 천년 마주해야 하는지.

시린 밤에 아무도 모르게
가물거리는 바람 한줄기
하늘과 땅을 흔들어 깨운다.

너에게서 빛나는 눈빛을 본다.
어느 것 하나라도 버릴 게 없다.

너에게로 바람길 더듬어 안기면
나도 한떨기 별이 된다.

# The monologue of stars

For a thousand years' going at the speed of light,
I heard that the stars in the night sky would still be shining
Have that stars run over to me for a thousand years?
Have I come closer for a thousand years from my previous life?

Maybe
Should we face us for a thousand years until the next life?

On a chilly night secretly
A wisp of flickering wind,
Awakens the sky and the ground.

I can see your shining eyes
There is nothing to throw away.

When I am hugged by you with groping a windy road
I become a bunch of stars too.

# 연기

마지막 한恨으로 형상하는
너의 선線
수선한 향방을
절망으로 비롯하는 의미.

네 넓이로
이역異域의 자락을 여미어
시원始原에 이르른다.

시간은 파장터에서
때 늦게 넘어온 바람
허물어진 구름의 층계.

나는 우주 한가운데로
새로이 떠나간다.

# Smoke

What it forms an image with final deep sorrow
It's your line
The confused direction
Means the beginning of despair.

With your width
Closing tightly the edge of different areas
Reaches the original area.

Time is the winds which come over later
From the closed market
It's the stairs of crumbled clouds.

Into the center of the universe
I am leaving afresh.

# 구름은 어디로 가서

꽃의 발돋움으로
기진맥진한 때에도
조금씩 가까이 다가왔다.

구름은 어디로 가서
으깨어진 그림자로 서성이다가
꿈으로 돌아오는가.

떠서 사는 구름으로
쥐어지지 않는 빛깔 속에서
나는 바람이 된다.

안개 속으로 사랑의 예감은
가끔씩 일그러진 채 돌아오지만
나는 일없이 노을 한자락이나 덮는다.

# Where do the clouds go

By the tiptoe of flowers
Even when exhausted
It comes closer little by little.

Where do the clouds go and
Linger with broken shadows,
Return to a dream?

As floating clouds
In the uncatchable color
I become winds.

The foreboding of love into the fog
Often returns as twisted
Unintentionally, I cover a piece of sunset.

# 장승 곁에서

장승이 눈 부릅뜨고 훑어본다.

빈틈없이 돌아가는 때마다
지난 일 하나라도
헛눈 팔지 않았는지.

구겨진 꽃잎
바람으로 둔갑하기도 하고
바람에 치이어 비틀거리다가
어떤 것은 무릎이 깨어지고
어떤 것은 땅바닥에 주저앉았다.

지금은
어둠 속에서 불티로
어디론지 휑하니 사라진다
사람의 침묵을 대신하여.

# Beside the totem pole

The totem pole looks through me with glaring eyes.

Whenever I return flawlessly
Wondering whether I did do
Any of the prior things lightly.

Crumpled petal is
Sometimes changed as the wind
Stumblingly hit by the wind
Some of the knees are broken
Some sat down on the ground.

Now
As fire-flake in the dark
Vacantly it's gone somewhere
On behalf of man's silence.

# 섬 사람 · 1

이 시대의
내 조국은
섬이다.

지도를 펴면
앞 모습은 바다요
뒷 모습은 절벽이다.

고구려 시대의
내 조국은
대륙이었다.

삼팔선을 하얗게 긋고
턱없이 못 가는
내 조국은
허공에 둥둥 떠 있는
차라리 섬이다.

## An islander · 1

In this age
My homeland is
An island.

When opening the map
The front is the sea
The backside is a cliff.

In the Koguryo era
My homeland was
A continent.

With the 38th parallel drawn white
Absurdly inapproachable
My homeland is
Floating in the air,
It's rather an island.

제 4 부 Part 4

# 따뜻한 중심에 이르는 길

# The Road to the Warm Center

산이 하는 말을
듣는다
거슬림이 없는 말이다.

산의 말은 침묵이다.
-「산은」 중에서

Hearing what the mountain says
It's a word without annoying

The word of a mountain is silence.
- The Part of 「The mountain is」

# 가는 길

진작 마음을 터놓고 있으면서도
표정까지 닫힌 것 같이 하고서
서로 마주 바라본다.

호수 속 하늘과 구름도
바람이 하는 일이 무엇인지
곁에서 지켜보고
아무 것에나 흡수되는 것인지
풋내가 가시면 과일이 될까.

이상스럽게 끓어오르는
그 무엇이 꺾이어
나의 한복판엔 언제나
무언가가 젖는다.

기적소리에 밤비가
손길만 휘젓고 있다.

## On my way

Already open-mindedly but
Pretending to be closed even face's expression,
Facing each other.

The sky and a cloud in the lake are
Watching it from the side
What does the wind do,
Whether it's absorbed by anything,
Whether it could be a fruit if it loses the fresh smell.

Strangely boiling
Something is broken
Always in my midst
Something gets wet.

After a train whistle, the night rain
Is just flapping its hands.

# 중심을 위하여

달빛 푸르는 호숫가

어디선가 낮은 목소리

나를 잔잔히 흔든다.

발목에 모아지는 힘살

중심을 세워야겠다.

# For my center

The lakeside with the moonlight blue

A low voice somewhere

Shake me gently.

Strength gathered at the ankle

I must build my center.

# 그리움의 무게

모진 거
그리움이여.

세월이란 게
누구에게나
비켜가는 게 아니라지만

삼십 년 만에 돌아온
내 의식 속의 동산은
무엇 하나 변한 게 없다.

텅 빈
그 속의
가득함이여.

꼬깃꼬깃 접힌 언어들을
연서戀書로 펴내어도
그리움의 무게는
날이 갈수록 더하다.

## The weight of longing

A severe thing
It's longing.

Time is
Not getting out of the way
To anyone.

The garden of my consciousness,
Which comes back after thirty years,
Has nothing to be changed.

Empty
Inside there
It's fullness.

The words folded crumply
Even pumping out it by a love letter
The weight of longing
Gets more day by day.

# 흔들림

오늘도
너로부터 깨어난다.

밤과 낮의 부끄러움이
나뭇가지의 흔들림으로 보인다.

가로등에 안개가 피어올라
새삼, 잃어버린 날을 그린다.

땅 위가 꽃밭이던 시절은
아득히 사라져가고

지금 이 자리는
다만 흔들림의 자리다.

# Shaking

Today, as well
I'm awakening from you.

The shyness of night and day,
Looks like the shaking of tree branches.

Fogs rise in the street lamp,
Yearn for a lost day anew.

The days when the ground was a flower garden
Been disappearing far away and

Now this place is
Just a spot of shaking.

# 허공에서

선잠 깨어
바스러져가는 나의 형상을 본다.

생색낼 무엇도 없는데
너에게 치장하고 싶은 건
이 한밤 뿐이다.

어둠에 기댄 몸부림,
모든 것이 갇혀버린 정지의 꼭대기에
나의 순간들을 널어 놓고
조금씩 나를 날리면
메아리로 되돌아오는 나를 만나본다.

손바닥에 꼭 쥐어진 허욕이
내 가슴을 부식시킨다.

너로부터 퍼져오는 향기가
내 시간의 목을 휘감는다
한밤을 사르는 동안에도
자신의 변형된 모습에서
그림자로 남은 나는
그래도 다시 비롯되는 꿈이었다.

# In the air

Awakened from light sleep
I see my vanishing image.

There's nothing to boast
What I want to decorate you with
Is only this midnight.

A struggle leaned into the dark,
At the stopped top where everything is trapped
I spread my memories
Blow me away little by little
Meet me returning as an echo.

The desire of vanity grabbed by the palm
Corrodes my heart.

The scent that comes from you
Wrap around the neck of my time
Even during burning the midnight
From the transformed shape of mine
I remained as a shadow,
Still was a dream that starts again.

# 방 황

무슨 까닭으로
홍수처럼 개울을 넘쳐
가슴마다 나부끼는지 알 수가 없습니다.

눈을 뜨면
햇살은 까맣게 파닥거리고
다만, 가위 눌린
중
량.

그래도
밤은
나를 옹호합니다.

나만의 정처없는 깃발이여.

# Wandering

For what reason
It overflows the stream like a flood and
Fluttering on each heart, I don't know that.

When opening my eyes
The sunshine is flapping in black
Just, have sleep paralysis
Heavy
Weight.

But still
The night
Stands up for me.

My merely driftless flag.

# 당신의 대답

당신은
나를 수습하는 신음입니다.

시골 하늘 자락에 크레용으로
당신을 덧칠합니다.

당신은 뒷걸음쳐서
현기어린 천성天性의 빗장을 풀어 줍니다.

이 밤 동안만은
당신처럼 앓습니다.

분홍 날개로
눈부신 햇빛의 언덕으로 오릅니다.

당신과 나의 하늘 속에서
비롯되는 먼동.

내가 모종한 세월은
당신의 대답이 됩니다.

# Your answer

You're
A moan of settling me.

With crayons on the edge of the country sky
I paint you over.

You step backward and
Unlatch the gate of faintish heavenly nature.

For this night only
I am sick like you.

With pink wings
I am soaring on the splendid hill of sunshine.

Inside the sky between you and me
Far dawn is beginning.

The years I've seeded
Become your answer.

# 산

처음
산은 내 안에서
벙그는 영혼의
푸르름이렸다.

산은
말이 없어도
그대로 나지막한
부름이렸다.

산은
맨살의 무게를 가늠하는
꽃으로 가득하니

산은 오로지
산꽃 속에 살렸다.

# A mountain

At first
A mountain inside me
Might be the blueness of
A spirit in a bud.

A mountain
Might be wordless but
Still low,
A calling.

A mountain
Has plenty of flowers
With guessing the weight of their bare skin.

A mountain
Will live only in the mountain flowers.

# 겨울 산

빈 가지 끝에
매달린 침묵을 그 누가 보아주기나 할까.

언제부터 언제까지
바람은 부름일까.

다 버리고도
무엇이 아직 남아 있는 걸까.

찬바람 앞세워
제 모습 허뜨리지 않는
겨울 산
그 아래 나의 이름은
회한으로 남았나 보다.

# The winter mountain

On the end of an empty branch
Who will show the silence hanging there?

From when to when,
May the wind be the calling?

All throw away then,
What still remains?

A cold wind ahead
Unbreaking its shape,
The winter mountain
Below it, my name might be
Left as remorse.

# 산은

산은 다만 초록만 남겨 놓고
갈색 바람이 둘러앉아
회의를 시작한다.

가지와 뿌리는
내밀한 연서戀書로 동화된다.

산 앞에선
삭이지 못하는 울화.

산이 하는 말을 듣는다
거슬림이 없는 말이다.

산의 말은 침묵이다.

# The mountain is

The mountain leaves only green
A brown wind sits around,
Start the meeting.

Branches and roots
Are assimilated into a secret love letter.

In front of the mountain
The anger cannot be settled.

Hearing what the mountain says
It's a word without annoying.

The word of a mountain is silence.

# 가로등

황혼은 진솔했다
비록 하늘 끝에 베인 낯선 정취로
생기를 찾았다 할지라도
안개가 깔리면
가로등은 일제히 눈을 뜬다
자기를 밝힌다.

안개는 비로소 사라진다
머리 위로 어둠은 짙어진다
하늘에 가로등이 얼비친다
땅 위 명암의 만남이다.

가로등은 서서히 밤을 태운다
가로등은 노랗게 빛난다
앙상한 나목들의 발목까지
떨어지는 그림자를 쓸어안는다.

깊은 밤엔
소복한 여인의 몸짓으로.

# The street lamps

The twilight is sincere
With an unfamiliar mood that's cut on the edge of the
sky
Even it recovers lively
When it gets foggy
The street lamps all open their eyes,
Lighten themselves.

Fogs finally disappear
The darkness deepens overhead
The street lamps dimly glimmer in the sky
It's a meeting of light and shade on the ground.

The street lamps burn the night slowly
The street lamps glow yellowy
To the ankle-deep of skinny bare trees
The falling shadows are embraced.

Deep in the night
As the gesture of a woman in white mourning clothes.

## 바람의 자리

눈을 감고
파도소리를 그린다.
이순耳順의 세월이 조급하다.
번민의 소용돌이에
차마 눈길을 돌릴 수 없다.

속마음 하나씩 고른다.
맨발로 비탈을 오르던 바람
신나게 어디론가 내달릴 바람
아직도 모르는 그 어디로
지쳐서 휘둘리며 달리는 바람

하다못해 꿈도 날리고
마냥 둥둥 떠서
어디로 아득히 달려가려는가.

이슬 머금은 지평에
또 내일의 자리를 받을런지.

# The seat of the winds

I close my eyes and
Long for the sound of the waves
The years of sixty are hasty
In the whirlpool of anxiety,
Can't bear to turn my eyes.

I choose the inner mind one by one.
The wind that climbed on the slope with bare feet
The wind that will run somewhere excitingly
To someplace still unknown
The wind that runs staggeringly by fatigue.

Blowing away even the last dreams
Floating away simply
Where will it run far away?

On the dewy horizon,
Could it get again the seat for tomorrow?

# 빗소리를 듣는다

빗소리 속에서
고섶엣 것도 생각해 내지 못하는구나.

해꼬지 없이, 비굴함 없이
등신 몸짓으로
같은 얼굴을 가지고도
그렇게 다르게 살았구나.

잠을 설치고
어디론가 안개 속의
열린 통로를 따라나왔다.

회한으로 남은 시간
이젠 정작 모두 잊어버리자.

오늘도 하룻내
일없이 빗소리를 듣는다.

## Hearing the raining sound

In the raining sound
I can't remember even the front thing that's placed to find easily.

Without harmfulness, without humiliation
With a foolish gesture
With the same face but
I lived so differently.

Sleep fitfully
Somewhere in a mist,
Come out through open passage.

Left times remorsefully
Let's forget really all now.

All day today
Hearing the raining sound to no purpose.

# 비탈에 선 나무

벼랑 위에 홀씨 하나 날아와
돌 틈새 나무로
푸르게 자라고 있다.

포근한 햇살에
가지 흔들거린다.

비탈 새끼손가락만한 돌 틈새로 뻗은 뿌리
돌에 맺히는 습기로 젖어 산다.

매무새 허술한 나무
봄여름을 보내고

허공을 휘젓는 나뭇가지
가을 가고
겨울이다.

# The standing tree on the slope

A seed flies over the cliff
As a tree in a stone crack,
Been growing greenish.

Warm, full sunshine,
The branches are swaying.

The root stretched into a stone crack as tiny as a little finger,
It lives in moisture that forms on the stone.

The tree with the poor appearance of a dress,
Spent spring and summer.

A branch that stirs in the air
The autumn is over
It's winter.

# 고백에 대하여

밤새 흐느낌의 음성
알아들을 수는 없어도
언뜻 스치는 예감으로
누구인지를 알았지.

목이 매이는 일들이
어찌 죽음을 지켜보는 이의 마음뿐이랴.

부모님 병 수발 몇 밤에
기진맥진해진 삶이여.

부모님 편하실 때
시집이나 갈 일이지
괜시리 센 고집 틀어잡고
이제 와서
오장 뒤집은들 무슨 소용이 있겠는가.

그 맥빠진 목소리
이제 철이 드는 절규가 아니런가.

# Regarding confession

The sobbing voice all night
Even incomprehensible
As a premonition swiftly passing,
Able to know who it is.

Watching someone's passing away
How can it be the only thing among the indescribable incidents?

After a few days of caring for parents' illness
The exhausting life it is.

When parents were healthy
Should have married a man,
Uselessly grabbed the strong stubbornness
Here now
What's the use of five viscera overturned?

That feeble voice
Now it's maybe the crying of maturing.

鄭松田 시인

- 1962년 「시와 시론」으로 등단.
- 서라벌예술대학 문예창작과 졸.
- 중앙대학교 국문과 및 동 대학원 졸.
- 용인시 죽전중학교 교장, 한라대학교, 경기대학교 겸임교수 역임.
- 세계시문학회 회장 역임.
- 한국자유시인협회 본상, 세계시문학상 대상, 경기도문학상 대상, 경기예술 대상, 현대 시인상 수상.
- 한국현대시인협회 지도위원, 한국작가협회 최고위원.
- 한국현대시인협회, 세계시문학회, 미당 시맥회 회원.

■ 시집

「그리움의 무게」, 「바람의 침묵」, 「꽃과 바람」, 「빛의 울림을 그린다」, 「내 이렇게 살다가」, 「바람의 말」.

■ 자작시 감상 선집

「그리움과 사랑의 되풀이」, 「자연과 우주의 너울」, 「내 삶의 소용돌이」, 「내 인생의 뒤안길」.

■ 한영시집

「숨은 꽃」, 「너를 맞아 보낸다」, 「꽃과 아내」, 「너와의 걸음걸이」

# Poet Song-jun Jung

- Debuted with 「Poems and Poetics」 in 1962
- Graduated Literary Creation from Seorabeol University of Arts
- Received and graduated master's degree from Joong-ang University
- School president of Jukjeon Middle School in Yong-in City. Served as affiliated professor of Hanla University and Kyeongki University
- Served as the president of Literary Society of the World Poetry
- Awardee of Korea Free Poet Association, first line up at World Poetry Literature Award, first line up at Kyeonggido Literature Award, first line up at Kyeonggi Art Award, the receipient of the Modern Poet Award.
- Direction committee of Korea Modern Poet Association, the executive committee of Korea Author Association
- Member of Korea Modern Poset Association, World Poet Literary Society, and Midang Poet Line Association

■ Collections of Poems

「The weight of longing」, 「The silence of the wind」,
「Flower and wind」, 「Drawing the echo of lights」,
「Iliving in such way」, 「The words of the wind」.

■ Collection of poems for appreciation

「Repetition of longing and love」, 「The swell of nature and universe」, 「Whirlpool of my life」, 「Backwaters of my life」.

■ Korean-English Poems

「The hidden flower」, 「Sending you after meeting you」,
「Flowers and my wife」, 「Walking with you」

정송전 한영시집 *1*

# 숨은 꽃

2022년 8월 18일 1판 1쇄 인쇄
2022년 8월 22일 1판 1쇄 발행

지은이 | 정송전
펴낸이 | 김효열

펴낸곳 | **을지출판공사**

등록번호 | 1985 년 2 월 14 일 제 2-741 호
주　　소 | 서울시 마포구 양화진길 41, 603호
우편번호 | 04083
대표전화 | 02) 334-4050
팩시밀리 | 02) 334-4010
전자우편 | ejp4050@hanmail.net

값 12,000원

ISBN 978-89-7566-214-0　　03810

Korean-English Poems Collection of Jeong Song Jeon 1

# The hidden flower

1st edition printed August 18, 2022
1st edition published August 22, 2022

Author Jeong Song Jeon
Publisher Kim Hyo Yeol

Published EulJi Publishing Company

Registration 1985. 2. 14 No. 2-741
Address 603. 41, Yanghwajin-gil, Mapo-go, Seoul, Korea
Phone 02-334-4050 Fax 02-334-4010
e-mail ejp4050@hanmail.net

Value 12,000 won

---

ISBN 978-89-7566-214-0 03810